DATE DUE

			PRINTED IN U.S.A.

A CENTURY OF *Flavor*

NIELSEN-MASSEY VANILLAS

A CENTURY OF

Flavor

NIELSEN-MASSEY VANILLAS

A CENTURY OF *Flavor*

NIELSEN-MASSEY VANILLAS

Published by Nielsen-Massey Vanillas, Inc.

Copyright © 2008 by
Nielsen-Massey Vanillas, Inc.
1550 Shields Drive
Waukegan, IL 60085-8307
800-525-7873
www.nielsenmassey.com

Food photography © by Steven Paul Lalich
Archival photography © by Nielsen-Massey Vanillas, Inc.

Food Photography: Steve Lalich/Lalich Photography
Food and Prop Stylist: Julee Rauch
Food Stylist and Consulting Chef: Susan Lalich
Project Manager: Vicki Gawlinski
Food Technologist: Ann Juttelstad

Library of Congress Control Number: 2007929848
ISBN: 978-0-9795991-0-1

Edited, Designed, and Manufactured by
Favorite Recipes® Press
An imprint of

FRP.

P.O. Box 305142
Nashville, Tennessee 37230
1-800-358-0560

Art Direction: Steve Newman and Starletta Polster
Book Designer: Sheri Ferguson
Project Editor: Susan Larson

Printed in China
First Printing 2008

MISSION STATEMENT

Quality and excellence is the foundation for the management of our business and the basis for our goal of customer satisfaction.

Nielsen-Massey Vanillas is dedicated to providing the best pure vanilla and flavor extract products free of defects which will satisfy our present customers and future customers, on time, all the time.

1907 – 2007

100 Years

NIELSEN · MASSEY VANILLAS

FOREWORD

I live near Nielsen-Massey's plant where they produce vanilla extract, not because of my ongoing love affair with the fragrant, alluring vanilla pod made through the care and nurturing of the only fruit-bearing orchid in the world . . . by sheer luck. A favorite of kings and queens, its attraction has continued from royalty right into the kitchens of notable chefs as well as great home cooks.

Exotic vanilla orchids are grown and hand-pollinated halfway across the world, near the equator. The long green beans are then harvested, fermented, dried in the sun, carried to market to be sold, and then bought and brought to the Midwest to be placed in the hands of the finest extract producers in the country, Nielsen-Massey. These Vanilla Specialists are the best at it and have been for three generations. When I need to know anything about vanilla, I run to the Nielsen family.

Since 1907 the family has been making flavorings in the purest, most natural way. Their cold extraction process gently extracts the complex flavor components (more than 300!) from the vanilla beans and then preserves them in jewel-like bottles to be sold for flavoring dishes from delicate pastries to sauces for lobster. No imitation flavoring could possibly replicate the complexity of 300 different flavor compounds, some of which have yet to be identified. Their innovative products, including vanilla powder, vanilla bean paste, beans, and many flavors of extracts including chocolate, lemon, almond, coffee, and orange, make them the leader in their field.

This deliciously interesting cookbook combines recipes from the Nielsen family collection as well as recipes from chef friends attracted by Nielsen-Massey's quality. It has a delightful collection of bakery and pastry recipes and also teaches you how vanilla can be essential in savory dishes. Vanilla can be as important in Crème Brûlée or Lemon-Pistachio Biscotti as it is in Apricot Mango BBQ Ribs or Creamy Vanilla Sweet Potatoes.

So crack open this book and crack open a bottle of Nielsen-Massey and start creating magic. But don't forget to share what you make . . . that's the best part!

—*Gale Gand*
EXECUTIVE PASTRY CHEF/PARTNER, TRU AND CENITARE RESTAURANTS
HOST OF "SWEET DREAMS," FOOD NETWORK
COOKBOOK AUTHOR

TABLE OF
Contents

MASSEY & MASSEY CO. CERTAINLY MAKE FINE VANILLA.

Greetings

At Nielsen-Massey Vanillas, we are thrilled to be celebrating our Centennial Anniversary. We appreciate the confidence the public has placed in us and thank you for being a part of our flavorful history.

The company was founded in 1907 as Massey's by Otis Kline and Richard Massey to provide aromas for the cleaning industry. With the shared leadership of Richard Massey and Chatfield Nielsen Sr., Massey's became Vanilla Specialists, providing all types of vanillas and flavors to primarily food manufacturers. Under the guidance of Chatfield Sr., the company name was changed to Nielsen-Massey Vanillas. With the second generation leadership of Chatfield Jr., the company evolved into Pure Vanilla Specialists, as the focus was placed on just all-natural, pure vanillas. In other significant moves, Nielsen-Massey also entered the retail as well as international markets during his tenure. New, innovative products—Pure Vanilla Powder, Pure Vanilla Bean Paste and Certified Organic Vanillas—were developed to enhance our tradition of quality products during Camilla Nielsen's management. In 1995 Camilla opened Nielsen-Massey Vanillas International in Leeuwarden, the Netherlands, to better service our world audience. Presently Craig, Beth, and Matt Nielsen, the third generation, continue the legacy and have revisited the company's roots by developing a new product line of pure flavor extracts complimentary to our highly respected pure vanilla products. We continue to grow internationally and nationally as each day brings new challenges and greater opportunities to pursue continued excellence.

We are a family business, now in our third generation of ownership. Our employees share in our success thereby creating a proprietary interest in the vanillas and flavor extracts. We continue an old-fashioned attitude toward business—a belief in hard work, dedication, and integrity. Becoming an empire or part of another's empire is not in our business plan, as we better serve our customers as we are. By purchasing the highest-quality vanilla beans available and utilizing our unique cold extraction process, we slowly extract the delicate flavoring matter from the vanilla beans to provide you with a true vanilla bouquet.

We are Vanilla Specialists. There is something distinctive about being a specialist. We simply do a better job. We produce quality. Whether used in sweet or savory applications, we provide only the finest products and deliver only the best in service. Companies have relied on our superior, prompt, and cost-effective product since 1907. We have confidence that we will continue to focus on the quality you desire and expect from Nielsen-Massey Vanillas.

Best wishes and flavorful cooking . . .

— *The Nielsen Family*

◀ *Vintage tradeshow exhibit, circa 1930*

ACKNOWLEDGMENTS

We hope that you will enjoy *A Century of Flavor* as much as we enjoyed creating it. Although there are many people to thank, we would like to name a few who made this possible.

We thank Otis Kline and Richard Massey, for without them starting the company in 1907, none of this may have occurred. This book is dedicated to the memory of our father, Chatfield Nielsen Jr., for without his passion and love for vanilla and vision for the future, we would not be celebrating our Centennial Anniversary. He started and drove the process which turned a struggling flavor company into a leading producer of pure vanilla recognized internationally for its quality. It is also dedicated to our mother, Camilla Nielsen, who after Chat's death, stepped into the leadership role of the company and continued the direction and vision initiated by him.

We owe a deep debt of gratitude to the chefs and friends who contributed recipes to the book. We thank the following for their fantastic submissions: Chefs Rick Bayless, Ina Pinckney, Biagio Settepani, and J. Warren, as well as our friends at the French Pastry School, Marcy Goldman, and Todd Eller. We also greatly appreciate the wonderful foreword written by Chef Gale Gand.

We would like to thank our friends at Lalich Photography who helped us throughout the process of developing this book. Their excellent photography brought these recipes to life. Also, thank you to the people at FRP® who provided the guidance to help Vanilla Specialists (who know little about publishing, but a great deal about vanilla) develop this cookbook.

Finally, we would be remiss if we did not thank our customers, suppliers, and employees, for without their support over the last 100 years, none of this would have happened.

So, as our late father always said, please "Use and Enjoy!"

—Craig, Beth, and Matt Nielsen

Chatfield Nielsen, Jr.

11

INTRODUCTION

When it comes to making pure vanilla, no one does it quite like Nielsen-Massey Vanillas.

Established in 1907, Nielsen-Massey Vanillas, Inc. has become known as the producer of the finest vanilla both in the United States and internationally. This family-owned and family-managed business takes pride in the quality products it produces, its people, and its customers.

Those who demand these quality products include manufacturers of premium ice creams and novelties, confectioners, bakers, chefs of fine restaurants, and the home cook. Gourmet food shops and fine grocers stock Nielsen-Massey's products on their shelves for discriminating consumers who appreciate the art of fine cooking and baking. Whether bought by the large industrial user or purchased at retail for a batch of the very best cookies, Nielsen-Massey's Pure Vanillas and Pure Flavors are sought for their quality, flavor, and varied functionality.

Although vanilla is the heart and foundation of Nielsen-Massey Vanillas, responding to their customers' needs has led them to explore new product arenas. Nielsen-Massey is now offering a line of new Pure Flavor Extracts which include: Pure Chocolate Extract, Pure Almond Extract, Pure Orange Extract, Pure Lemon Extract, Pure Coffee Extract, Orange Blossom Water, and Rose Water. As with all Nielsen-Massey products, these are produced within the strictest quality standards.

Globally, Nielsen-Massey meets the demand for its products from its corporate headquarters located in Waukegan, Illinois, USA, and with production facilities in both Waukegan and Nielsen-Massey Vanillas International in Leeuwarden, the Netherlands. Between these two facilities, Nielsen-Massey serves markets in North America, South America, Central America, Australia, New Zealand, the Pacific Rim, Europe, Africa and the Middle East.

Nielsen-Massey is audited annually by the American Institute of Baking, from whom it has received the highest ranking awarded, a Superior rating, each year since 1990. All Nielsen-Massey's vanilla products are certified Kosher and Gluten-free, and they have been a certified Organic producer since 1997.

From its ever-popular Madagascar Bourbon Pure Vanilla Extract to creating custom blends and flavors for specific customer needs, Nielsen-Massey has earned the reputation as makers of the finest extracts in the world.

An exciting new era for the company is underway as more product introductions are planned and the family oversees the expansion of the business. As Nielsen-Massey Vanillas continues to grow, the company remains mindful of its flavorful past and looks forward to a tasteful future.

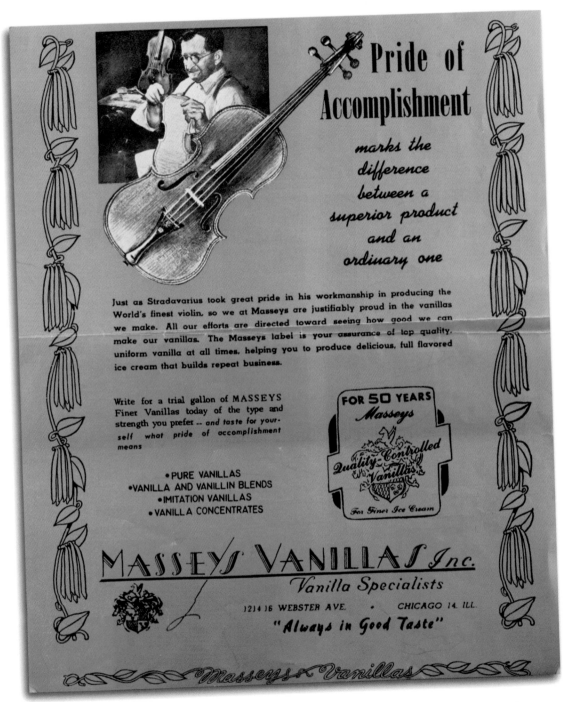

Pride of Accomplishment

marks the difference between a superior product and an ordinary one

Just as Stradavarius took great pride in his workmanship in producing the World's finest violin, so we at Masseys are justifiably proud in the vanillas we make. All our efforts are directed toward seeing how good we can make our vanillas. The Masseys label is your assurance of top quality, uniform vanilla at all times, helping you to produce delicious, full flavored ice cream that builds repeat business.

Write for a trial gallon of MASSEYS Finer Vanillas today of the type and strength you prefer -- *and taste for yourself what pride of accomplishment means*

- PURE VANILLAS
- VANILLA AND VANILLIN BLENDS
- IMITATION VANILLAS
- VANILLA CONCENTRATES

FOR 50 YEARS
Masseys
Quality-Controlled Vanillas
For Finer Ice Cream

MASSEYS VANILLAS Inc.
Vanilla Specialists

1214-16 WEBSTER AVE. • CHICAGO 14, ILL.

"Always in Good Taste"

Masseys Vanillas

"Pride of Accomplishment" ad 1957

TESTIMONIALS

"Cream-of-the-crop Nielsen-Massey Vanillas reaches their centennial—a veritable milestone in the vibrant history of the vanilla bean. This sweet taste of historical success puts Nielsen-Massey Vanillas firmly at the front of the house. When it comes to raising the bar, they have led the pack. Perfect partners, presenting a centenary of distilled full-flavored culinary perfection—I for one say, 'bravo, encore, and a hundred more!'"

—KERRY VINCENT, SHOW DIRECTOR, AUTHOR,
WEDDING-CAKE DESIGNER, AND HALL OF FAME SUGAR ARTIST

"Baking and dessert production demands high-quality products for its formulations. For over two decades, I have been using Nielsen-Massey Vanillas products for specialty desserts and international competitions that require winning recipes. This quality product, combined with fantastic service and a personal approach, is a winning formula!"

—STANTON HO, CORPORATE EXECUTIVE CHEF
CHOCOLATES À LA CARTE

"One of the dearest memories I have is walking through the door of a nondescript building in Chicago's Lincoln Park and being greeted warmly by the aroma of vanilla and Chat Nielsen. On that day, I needed —and could afford—my first gallon of Nielsen-Massey Vanilla. It was 1982, and we talked of how we would grow our businesses with integrity and love. And we did."

—INA PINKNEY, CHEF, OWNER INA'S RESTAURANT, CHICAGO

TESTIMONIALS

"

Vanilla is an aromatic, delectable ingredient essential to all elements of pastry. I am grateful for this magnificent product in its many different forms as well as the continuous education that has been provided to the industry by this remarkable family for over one hundred years."

—ANIL ROHIRA, CORPORATE PASTRY CHEF, ALBERT USTER IMPORTS

"

As a professional pastry chef and baker, creating recipes that are alive with flavor and inspire the senses is what outstanding baking is all about.

Since day one of my professional baking career, I have depended on the vanilla experts, Nielsen-Massey, for a palette of pure vanilla extracts, each uniquely suited to incredible scones, biscotti, cookies, cakes, or pastries. In short, Nielsen-Massey Vanillas have been the very soul and anchor of my recipes, enhancing the baker's craft bite by beautiful bite.

Tastes have changed since Nielsen-Massey first began, but the preference and acknowledgment of quality and purity by the vanilla 'kings' has never gone out of style. Congratulations!"

—MARCY GOLDMAN, PASTRY CHEF, MASTER BAKER, COOKBOOK AUTHOR
AND JULIA CHILD AWARD NOMINEE

"

Nielsen-Massey Vanillas has been part of my pantry since I started baking professionally twenty years ago. I can't imagine using anything else. It's trusted and true like my favorite recipes. The delicate yet full aroma adds a quality to my baked goods that can't be matched."

—EMILY LUCHETTI, COOKBOOK AUTHOR, EXECUTIVE PASTRY CHEF
FARALLON RESTAURANT, SAN FRANCISCO

VANILLA EQUIVALENCIES

Nielsen-Massey Vanilla Products can be used interchangeably depending on your preference, availability, or application. Here are a few quick tips to remember when using our vanilla products:

**One whole Vanilla Bean = one tablespoon Pure Vanilla Bean Paste =
one tablespoon Pure Vanilla Extract = one tablespoon Pure Vanilla Powder**

If a recipe calls for oranges, lemons, almonds, coffee, or chocolate, try substituting one of the Pure Flavor Extracts: Orange, Lemon, Almond, Coffee, or Chocolate.

STORAGE & USAGE TIPS

- Pure Extracts, Vanilla Bean Paste, Vanilla Powder, and Vanilla Beans should be stored in an airtight container at room temperature. They should not be subjected to freezing temperatures and should be kept away from direct sunlight.

- Keep in mind that extracts can not only add flavor, but complement and enhance other flavors—try it in combination with other flavors.

- For best results when using our extracts, add them at the end of the cooking process or cream them with butter for baking.

PRODUCT DESCRIPTIONS

Each variety of pure vanilla and pure flavor extract has its own particular attributes, flavor notes, and aromas, adding their own dimension and character to the foods in which they are used. The following are brief descriptions of each product used in our recipes as well as some suggested uses.

Madagascar Bourbon Pure Vanilla Extract, the pinnacle of vanillas, is an overall versatile vanilla with a rich, creamy, mellow flavor and velvety after-tones. It is ideal for general baking and cooking—sweet or savory. It is, of course, perfect in cakes, cookies, and pastries. It adds a touch of sweetness to succulent seafood sauces or marinades and cuts the acidity of tangy tomato sauces.

Madagascar Bourbon Pure Vanilla Bean Paste, with real vanilla seeds, is a secret way to be able to add more delicious vanilla flavor without thinning out your batters or sauces. It is ideal for recipes where you want to showcase the vanilla flavor and add eye appeal at the same time.

Madagascar Bourbon Pure Vanilla Powder is the essence of Madagascar Bourbon Pure Vanilla in a sugar-free powder base. It is ideal for cookies and baked goods. Use it in liquid or color-sensitive recipes like vanilla icings or as a flavoring for beverages, including coffee and tea. It is alcohol-free and dissolves instantly.

Madagascar Bourbon Gourmet Vanilla Beans are moist, flavorful beans that can be used for many cooking and baking applications. Simply split the bean and scrape the seeds into the dish. Use the seeds to attain a rich, creamy flavor, or simmer the whole bean in milk, cream, or other liquid before adding to recipes. The bean can then be rinsed, dried, and used again until the flavor has been depleted.

Madagascar Bourbon Pure Vanilla Sugar is the essence of Madagascar Bourbon Pure Vanilla infused with gourmet sugar. Use it in any product where a hint of vanilla and the sweetness of sugar are desired. It is ideal for adding an extra layer of pure flavor to baked goods such as cookies, cakes, pies, pastries, and much more! Pure Vanilla Sugar is also great for cooking, adding to beverages, or as a sweet topping.

Organic Madagascar Bourbon Pure Vanilla Extract, Organic Pure Vanilla Powder, or **Organic Whole Vanilla Beans** can be used in place of any of the other vanilla extracts, powder, or beans in the same manner, ensuring a natural and organic ingredient with pure vanilla flavor.

Tahitian Pure Vanilla Extract is distinctly unique from the other vanilla extracts. It has fruity, anisic notes that enhance fruit dishes such as cranberry sauce or cherries jubilee. This delicate flavor is best used in recipes that do not require high heat, such as refrigerated and frozen desserts, pastry creams, fruit pies and sauces, smoothies, shakes, puddings, or custards.

Tahitian Gourmet Vanilla Beans are plump, moist, flavorful beans that offer the same fruity, floral notes of the Tahitian Pure Vanilla Extract. Use in the same manner as any other variety of whole vanilla bean for a variety of cooking and baking applications. Scrape and use the seeds or simmer in liquid, then add to your recipe for a uniquely delicious vanilla flavor.

Mexican Pure Vanilla Extract offers a deep, spicy flavor. It spices up citrus fruits such as lemons, limes, and oranges and can also mellow out the bitterness of dark chocolate. It cuts the acidity and smooths out the heat in spicy or tomato-based dishes. Try it in cookies, cakes, frozen desserts, barbecue and spaghetti sauces, and salsas.

PRODUCT DESCRIPTIONS

Mexican Gourmet Vanilla Beans are moist, flavorful beans with the deep, spicy notes of the Mexican Pure Vanilla Extract. Use in the same manner as any other variety of whole vanilla bean for a variety of cooking and baking applications. Scrape and use the seeds or simmer in liquid, then add to your recipe for delicious vanilla flavor.

Pure Orange Extract is the perfect partner to vanilla, chocolate, strawberries, pineapples, and many other foods. Enhance rice, chicken, and fish dishes, even jams and marmalades. Add an orange burst to fruit pies, salad dressings, cream and custard desserts, and of course ice cream, sherbets, beverages, and pastries.

Pure Lemon Extract complements just about any dish! It has a special affinity for vanilla, orange, almond, and many other flavors. It's a natural with fish, pork, and chicken and it marries well with a variety of herbs such as parsley, rosemary, thyme, garlic, and basil. Lemon extract can be added to anything from beverages and vegetables to desserts and jellies.

Pure Chocolate Extract offers a rich and smooth chocolate flavor without sweetness. It pairs well with vanilla, almonds, cinnamon, coffee, nuts, raspberries, maple, mint, coconut, cream, cherries, and bananas. Add a whisper of chocolate to a wide variety of foods—from cakes, cookies, and icings to coffee, custards, and puddings.

Pure Almond Extract blends well with a host of foods and flavors including vanilla, chocolate, caramel, apples, coconut, cherries, cream, strawberries, raisins, and more. Add the warm, mellow, nutty flavor of almonds to pies and pastries, confections, frostings, and fillings for a fabulous finishing touch. Add it to dishes using almonds to enhance the almond flavor.

Pure Coffee Extract is the essence of rich brewed coffee in a concentrated form. Use it to add subtle richness to a vanilla milkshake or hot chocolate. Add it to vanilla yogurt, to hot fudge sauce as a topping for ice cream, or blend it into whipped cream to go with brownies or pound cake. It's also a great addition to molten chocolate cakes, tiramisu, or molasses cookies

Orange Blossom Water is made from a distillate of the Seville bitter orange from Spain and the Middle East. Used in Persian, Arabic, Indian, and Turkish dishes, Orange Blossom Water brings the sweet perfume of the orange grove to a variety of dishes. It is a delicious flavoring for custards and puddings, cakes and cookies, candies, and other confections. It complements vanilla, almond, cream, lemon, and other citrus flavors. Orange Blossom Water can even be a calming restorative when spritzed into the air.

Rose Water is a steam distillate made from the purest rose petals. Its delicate floral notes are perfect additions to Middle Eastern, Indian, and Greek foods such as baklava or rice puddings and are wonderful accents to delicate French pastry glazes and creams. Rose Water can flavor sugars and cookies for tea time and can be served as a beverage in sweetened hot water. Rose Water has an affinity for vanilla, cream, white chocolate, rice, and mild cheeses such as Brie or cream cheese.

All Nielsen-Massey products are Kosher and Gluten-Free Certified.

Curing vanilla beans in Mexico

on the side

SPA SALAD WITH ALMOND VINAIGRETTE

Toss the spinach, onion, 1 cup strawberries and 1/2 cup almonds gently in a large bowl. Pour the vinaigrette over the salad and toss to combine. Garnish with additional strawberries and almonds.

SERVES 2

10	OUNCES BABY SPINACH LEAVES, TORN INTO BITE-SIZE PIECES
1/2	RED ONION, THINLY SLICED
1	CUP STRAWBERRIES, THINLY SLICED
1/2	CUP SLICED ALMONDS
~	ALMOND VINAIGRETTE (BELOW)
~	ADDITIONAL STRAWBERRIES AND ALMONDS FOR GARNISH

ALMOND VINAIGRETTE

Whisk the Dijon mustard, syrup, vanilla extract, almond extract, salt and white pepper in a bowl. Add the canola oil in a fine stream, whisking constantly until incorporated. This will emulsify your salad dressing and it will not separate. Add the vinegar slowly, whisking constantly.

Note: Emulsified liquids are generally unmixable and whisking them together gradually will force them to combine.

MAKES 3/4 CUP

2	TEASPOONS DIJON MUSTARD
2	TEASPOONS PURE MAPLE SYRUP
1	TEASPOON NIELSEN-MASSEY MADAGASCAR BOURBON PURE VANILLA EXTRACT
1/4	TEASPOON NIELSEN-MASSEY PURE ALMOND EXTRACT
1/4	TEASPOON SALT
1/8	TEASPOON WHITE PEPPER
1/2	CUP CANOLA OIL
1/4	CUP NATURAL RICE VINEGAR

For added depth and character, add Pure Almond Extract to any nut bread, pumpkin bread, or banana bread.

23

VANILLA-INFUSED BALSAMIC VINAIGRETTE

I	TABLESPOON SPICY BROWN MUSTARD
2	TABLESPOONS HONEY
1/2	TEASPOON NIELSEN-MASSEY TAHITIAN PURE VANILLA EXTRACT
1/4	TEASPOON SALT
1/8	TEASPOON WHITE PEPPER
1/2	CUP LIGHT OLIVE OIL
I	TABLESPOON BALSAMIC VINEGAR
I	TABLESPOON NATURAL RICE VINEGAR

Whisk the brown mustard, honey, vanilla extract, salt and white pepper in a bowl. Add the olive oil in a fine stream, whisking constantly until incorporated. This will emulsify your salad dressing and it will not separate (see note page 23). Add the vinegars slowly, whisking constantly.

Use over fresh baby salad greens, or as a marinade for chicken, fish, pork or vegetables.

MAKES 3/4 CUP

Use Tahitian Pure Vanilla only in dishes that will not be exposed to high heat, as it will lose some of its delicate flavor.

GOLDEN SQUASH BISQUE

Preheat the oven to 375 degrees. Place the squash in a covered baking dish with the water. Bake for 30 minutes or until fork tender.

Melt the butter in a large saucepan over medium-low heat. Add the onion and sauté until golden brown. Whisk in the flour until blended. Add 1 1/2 cups chicken stock gradually, whisking constantly. Add the squash, salt and white pepper. Mash with a potato masher. Add the bay leaf and sage leaves. Simmer for 1 hour, stirring occasionally.

Remove the bay leaf and sage leaves. Spoon the squash mixture into a blender. Add the warm cream a little at a time, puréeing after each addition. Add the orange extract. Pour into the saucepan and reheat thoroughly. If the bisque is too thick, you may change the consistency by adding additional stock 1/4 cup at a time.

SERVES 4 TO 6

2	ACORN SQUASH, PEELED AND QUARTERED (ABOUT 2 CUPS)
3	TABLESPOONS WATER
3	TABLESPOONS BUTTER
1/4	CUP FINELY DICED ONION
1	TABLESPOON FLOUR
1 1/2	CUPS (OR MORE) ORGANIC CHICKEN STOCK
1	TEASPOON SALT
1/2	TEASPOON WHITE PEPPER
1	BAY LEAF
2	WHOLE FRESH SAGE LEAVES
1	CUP HEAVY WHIPPING CREAM, WARMED
1/2	TEASPOON NIELSEN-MASSEY PURE ORANGE EXTRACT

Add a few drops of Pure Orange Extract in cranberry juice to make a refreshing beverage.

FRESH BASIL-TOMATO SOUP WITH VANILLA

1/2 CUP FINELY DICED ONION

1/4 CUP FINELY DICED CARROTS

2 TABLESPOONS BUTTER

2 TABLESPOONS UNBLEACHED ALL-PURPOSE FLOUR

2 TEASPOONS DRIED ORGANIC ITALIAN SEASONING

2 CUPS (OR MORE) ORGANIC CHICKEN STOCK

1 (28-OUNCE) CAN PETITE DICED TOMATOES

1 1/2 TEASPOONS NIELSEN-MASSEY MADAGASCAR BOURBON PURE VANILLA EXTRACT

1/2 CUP FRESH BASIL, CHIFFONADE

1/2 TEASPOON SALT

1/4 TEASPOON WHITE PEPPER

1/2 CUP (2 OUNCES) FRESHLY GRATED PARMESAN CHEESE FOR GARNISH

Sauté the onion and carrots in the butter in a large saucepan until the onion is translucent. Stir in the flour and Italian seasoning until heated. Add 2 cups chicken stock gradually, stirring constantly. Stir in the tomatoes, vanilla extract, basil, salt and white pepper. Cover and simmer for 45 minutes, stirring occasionally. Add additional stock if desired and cook until heated through.

Ladle into soup bowls and garnish with the Parmesan cheese.

Note: A chiffonade refers to a method of stacking the basil leaves and finely shredding them with a sharp chef knife.

SERVES 4

There is none of the American liquor bourbon in Madagascar Bourbon Pure Vanilla. The name comes from the once French-owned Ile de Bourbon, or Bourbon Islands, of which Madagascar is the largest.

HEARTY WHITE BEAN CHILI

Heat the olive oil in a medium sauté pan over medium-high heat. Add the chicken and cook for 4 to 5 minutes or until brown. Remove the chicken from the pan with a slotted spoon and set aside. Add the onion to the sauté pan and cook until caramelized, stirring occasionally. Add the garlic and cook for 1 to 2 minutes. Pour in the chicken stock, scraping the bottom of the pan with a wooden spoon to deglaze.

Pour the stock mixture into a large saucepot and add the cooked chicken, tomatoes, tomato sauce, chiles, cumin, parsley, oregano, cayenne pepper and salt. Cover and simmer for 30 minutes, stirring occasionally. Add the chocolate extract and white kidney beans. Cook for 10 minutes.

Ladle the chili into soup bowls and garnish with the Parmesan cheese.

Note: Caramelization cooks the naturally occurring sugars in food and improves their flavor and appearance.

Deglaze means to stir a liquid, usually wine, in a sauté pan to loosen the cooked food particles from the pan.

Serves 6

2	TABLESPOONS OLIVE OIL
3	BONELESS SKINLESS CHICKEN BREASTS, MEDIUM DICE
1	CUP FINELY DICED ONION
4	GARLIC CLOVES, MINCED
1	CUP ORGANIC CHICKEN STOCK
1	(28-OUNCE) CAN DICED TOMATOES
1	(29-OUNCE) CAN TOMATO SAUCE
1	(7-OUNCE) CAN DICED GREEN CHILES
2	TEASPOONS GROUND CUMIN
2	TABLESPOONS DRIED ORGANIC PARSLEY
1	TABLESPOON DRIED ORGANIC OREGANO
1/4	TEASPOON CAYENNE PEPPER
1	TEASPOON KOSHER SALT
2	TEASPOONS NIELSEN-MASSEY PURE CHOCOLATE EXTRACT
1	(15-OUNCE) CAN WHITE KIDNEY BEANS, DRAINED
1/2	CUP (2 OUNCES) FRESHLY GRATED PARMESAN CHEESE

For a mellowing effect, add a couple drops of Nielsen-Massey Pure Chocolate Extract to hot salsa.

CARROTS WITH LEMON DILL BUTTER

1/4   CUP CLARIFIED BUTTER
2   TEASPOONS NIELSEN-MASSEY PURE
     LEMON EXTRACT
2   TEASPOONS MINCED FRESH DILL,
     OR 1 TEASPOON DRIED
     ORGANIC DILL
1/2   TEASPOON SALT
1/4   TEASPOON WHITE PEPPER
1   POUND CARROTS, SLICED

Whisk the clarified butter, lemon extract, dill, salt and white pepper in a large bowl. Add the carrots to the butter mixture and toss gently to coat. Place the carrots in a preheated large sauté pan. Sauté until tender-crisp. Serve warm.

Note: Clarified butter is melted, and the white milk solids are skimmed off the top, which allows the butter to be less heat sensitive and reduces the risk of burning.

SERVES 6 TO 8

Punch up the flavor of teas by adding a touch of Pure Lemon Extract.

CREAMY VANILLA SWEET POTATOES

Preheat the oven to 400 degrees. Wash the sweet potatoes and lightly coat the skins with canola oil. Pierce each potato several times with a fork. Place the potatoes on a foil-lined baking sheet. Bake for 1 hour or until fork tender.

Cut the hot potatoes into halves. Scoop the potato pulp into a mixing bowl, discarding the skins. Beat at medium speed for 1 minute using an electric mixer. Add the cream cheese, butter, syrup, vanilla extract, salt and pepper. Whip until creamy.

Spoon the whipped potatoes into six ramekins coated with nonstick cooking spray and top with the bacon. Place the ramekins on a baking sheet. Bake in a preheated 375-degree oven for 5 to 8 minutes or until heated through. Alternatively, they may be reheated in a microwave for 2 to 3 minutes.

SERVES 6

4	MEDIUM SWEET POTATOES
~	CANOLA OIL
2	OUNCES CREAM CHEESE, SOFTENED
1/2	CUP (1 STICK) BUTTER, SOFTENED
1/4	CUP REAL MAPLE SYRUP
1	TABLESPOON NIELSEN-MASSEY TAHITIAN PURE VANILLA EXTRACT
1/2	TEASPOON SALT
1/4	TEASPOON PEPPER
5	STRIPS BACON, CRISP-COOKED AND CRUMBLED

The reason why no synthetic can exactly match the true flavor of vanilla? Research shows that it is due to the complexity of the molecular makeup of the vanilla bean—not all of the compounds that contribute to the flavor and aroma of vanilla have been identified.

LEMON-BLEU STUFFED TOMATOES

2 TABLESPOONS DRY WHITE WINE

2 TEASPOONS FINELY
MINCED SHALLOTS

8 OUNCES CREAM CHEESE, SOFTENED

1 TEASPOON FINELY MINCED GARLIC

1/2 TEASPOON NIELSEN-MASSEY PURE
LEMON EXTRACT

1/8 TEASPOON WHITE PEPPER

1/4 TEASPOON CAYENNE PEPPER
(OPTIONAL)

5 OUNCES BLEU CHEESE CRUMBLES

2 PINTS CHERRY TOMATOES
(APPROXIMATELY 48)

Combine the wine and shallots in a small bowl. Let stand.

Combine the cream cheese, garlic, lemon extract, white pepper, cayenne pepper and shallot mixture in a mixing bowl. Beat until well blended using an electric mixer. Fold in the bleu cheese with a wooden spoon. Chill, covered, in the refrigerator.

Rinse the cherry tomatoes. Remove the tops by slicing a small amount off each tomato. Scoop out the seeds with a small measuring spoon. Cut a small slice off the bottom of each tomato so it will stand upright when plated. Fill each tomato with 1/2 tablespoon of the chilled Lemon-Bleu Stuffing using a pastry bag or spoon.

Note: You may use the stuffing as a gourmet appetizer on toasted slices of a French baguette topped with small cooked shrimp.

MAKES 24 TABLESPOONS OF STUFFING
FOR 48 TOMATOES

Oranges, lemons, and almonds all originated in Asia, but are now grown the world over for their flavor and aroma. The biggest almond producer is California.

LEMON AND ROSEMARY RISOTTO

Heat the chicken stock in a large microwave-safe measuring cup for 4 minutes on High. Set aside.

Heat the olive oil in a large sauté pan over medium heat. Add the rice and stir to coat. Reduce the heat to medium-low. Add 4 cups of the stock a little at a time, stirring constantly and cooking until the stock is absorbed after each addition. This will take approximately 30 to 40 minutes. The risotto will be creamy and yield to a gentle bite when done.

Stir in the parsley, rosemary, lemon extract, Parmesan cheese and enough of the remaining stock to maintain a creamy consistency.

SERVES 4

4   CUPS (OR MORE) ORGANIC
    CHICKEN STOCK
3   TABLESPOONS OLIVE OIL
1   CUP ARBORIO RICE
1/4 CUP MINCED FRESH
    ITALIAN PARSLEY
1   TABLESPOON MINCED FRESH
    ROSEMARY LEAVES
1/4 TEASPOON NIELSEN-MASSEY PURE
    LEMON EXTRACT
1/2 CUP (2 OUNCES) GRATED FRESH
    PARMESAN CHEESE

It normally takes five pounds of uncured, "green" vanilla beans to produce one pound of cured vanilla beans.

Vanilla mule train, Mexico

FILET MIGNON WITH VANILLA WINE SAUCE

For the sauce, combine the stock, wine, onion, marjoram, garlic, vanilla extract, tomato paste and brown sugar in a saucepan. Simmer until reduced by half. Strain through a fine mesh strainer into a small sauté pan. Whisk the butter into the sauce 1 tablespoon at a time over medium heat. The sauce will become glossy and slightly thickened.

For the steaks, preheat the oven to 400 degrees. Season the steaks with salt and pepper. Heat the olive oil in an oven-safe skillet over medium-high heat. Add the steaks and sear each side for 2 to 3 minutes. Place the skillet in the oven and roast for 8 to 10 minutes for medium or to the desired degree of doneness. Remove and let stand.

For the mushrooms, sauté the mushrooms in the clarified butter in a medium saucepan until brown.

To assemble, place the steaks on a serving platter. Spoon the sauce over the steaks. Garnish with the mushrooms.

SERVES 4

VANILLA WINE SAUCE

2	CUPS ORGANIC BEEF STOCK
1/4	CUP DRY RED WINE
1	SMALL ONION, SLICED IN HALF
3	LARGE SPRIGS OF FRESH MARJORAM OR OREGANO
2	WHOLE GARLIC CLOVES
1	TEASPOON NIELSEN-MASSEY ORGANIC MADAGASCAR BOURBON PURE VANILLA EXTRACT
1 1/2	TABLESPOONS TOMATO PASTE
1	TEASPOON LIGHT BROWN SUGAR
2	TABLESPOONS BUTTER, SOFTENED

STEAKS

4	(4-OUNCE) 1 1/2-INCH THICK STEAKS
~	SALT AND PEPPER TO TASTE
2	TABLESPOONS OLIVE OIL

MUSHROOMS

2	CUPS SLICED MUSHROOMS
1/4	CUP CLARIFIED BUTTER (SEE NOTE PAGE 32)

SAVORY PORK TENDERLOIN

1/3 CUP SOY SAUCE

1/4 CUP NATURAL RICE VINEGAR

2 TEASPOONS NIELSEN-MASSEY MADAGASCAR BOURBON PURE VANILLA EXTRACT

2 GARLIC CLOVES, MINCED

1 TEASPOON FRESHLY GROUND PEPPER

2 TEASPOONS DARK BROWN SUGAR

1 (3- TO 4-POUND) PORK TENDERLOIN, TRIMMED

Combine the soy sauce, vinegar, vanilla extract, garlic, pepper and brown sugar in a sealable plastic bag and mix well. Add the tenderloin and seal. Marinate in the refrigerator for 4 to 5 hours or overnight, turning the bag occasionally. Drain, discarding the marinade.

Grill the tenderloin over direct heat for 3 to 4 minutes on each side or until nicely seared. Grill over indirect medium heat for 35 to 45 minutes or to 145 degrees on a meat thermometer. For an accurate temperature, place the thermometer in the thickest part of the tenderloin. Place the pork on a plate and let stand; it will continue to cook as it stands. Pork should reach an internal temperature of 150 degrees.

SERVES 4

Each vanilla orchid is open for only part of one day and must be hand pollinated at that time, or a bean will not develop. Fortunately, the flowers do not all open on the same day, but over a period of about two months. Each vine is visited every day to check on the condition of the flowering.

APRICOT MANGO BBQ RIBS

For the rib seasoning, combine the chili powder, salt, garlic powder, cumin, thyme and olive oil in a bowl and mix well to make a paste. Rub evenly over the ribs. Wrap the ribs in plastic wrap and chill in the refrigerator for 2 hours or up to overnight.

For the sauce, combine the apricots, mangoes, chipotle chiles, brown sugar, garlic, olive oil, tomato paste, vanilla extract, vinegar, Worcestershire sauce, cumin, salt and cayenne pepper in a blender container and purée. Store in the refrigerator.

To bake the ribs, preheat the oven to 300 degrees. Unwrap the ribs and place on a rimmed baking sheet coated with nonstick cooking spray. Bake for 1 1/2 hours. Brush the sauce generously over the ribs. Bake for an additional 45 minutes or until the sauce caramelizes.

To grill the ribs, unwrap the ribs and place on a grill rack. Grill over indirect low heat for 1 1/2 hours. Brush the sauce generously over the ribs. Grill for an additional 1/2 hour.

Place the ribs on a foil-lined baking sheet. Cover with foil and let stand for 20 minutes. Successful grilling or baking of ribs occurs when ribs cook slowly over low temperatures.

SERVES 2 TO 4

RIB SEASONING
1 1/2 TABLESPOONS ANCHO CHILI POWDER
1 TEASPOON KOSHER SALT
1 TEASPOON ORGANIC GARLIC POWDER
1/2 TEASPOON CUMIN
1/2 TEASPOON GROUND THYME
2 TABLESPOONS EXTRA-VIRGIN OLIVE OIL
2 SLABS BABY BACK RIBS

APRICOT MANGO BBQ SAUCE
1/2 CUP MEDIUM DICED CANNED APRICOTS, DRAINED
1/2 CUP MEDIUM DICED FRESH OR JARRED MANGOES, DRAINED
1 (4-OUNCE) CAN MILD CHIPOTLE CHILES
2 TABLESPOONS DARK BROWN SUGAR
2 WHOLE GARLIC CLOVES
1 TABLESPOON OLIVE OIL
1 TABLESPOON TOMATO PASTE
2 TEASPOONS NIELSEN-MASSEY MADAGASCAR BOURBON PURE VANILLA EXTRACT
2 TEASPOONS BALSAMIC VINEGAR
1 TEASPOON WORCESTERSHIRE SAUCE
1 TEASPOON CUMIN
1/2 TEASPOON SALT
1/4 TEASPOON CAYENNE PEPPER (OPTIONAL)

DUCK BREAST WITH TAHITIAN POMEGRANATE CHUTNEY

TAHITIAN POMEGRANATE CHUTNEY

1	CUP 100% POMEGRANATE JUICE
2	TABLESPOONS SUGAR
1	TEASPOON Nielsen-Massey TAHITIAN PURE VANILLA EXTRACT
1/2	TEASPOON BALSAMIC VINEGAR
1	TART APPLE, PEELED AND DICED (ABOUT 1 CUP)
1	BOSC PEAR, PEELED AND DICED (ABOUT 1 CUP)
1/2	CUP COARSELY CHOPPED WALNUTS
1/2	CUP RAISINS

DUCK BREAST

4	DUCK BREASTS
~	SALT AND FRESHLY GROUND PEPPER

For the chutney, combine the juice, sugar, vanilla extract and vinegar in a large saucepan. Cook over medium heat until sugar is dissolved, stirring frequently. Add the apple, pear, walnuts and raisins. Cook for 5 to 8 minutes or until the fruit is tender, stirring frequently.

For the duck, preheat the oven to 400 degrees. Score the skin of each duck breast at a 45-degree angle approximately four times. Season with salt and pepper.

Preheat a large sauté pan over medium-high heat. Coat with nonstick cooking spray. Place the duck breasts skin side down in the pan. Sear for 4 minutes. Turn and sear for an additional 2 minutes.

Place a wire rack in a 9×13-inch roasting pan and coat the rack with nonstick cooking spray. Place the duck on the rack. Roast for 10 to 15 minutes or to the desired degree of doneness. Plate with the Tahitian Pomegranate Chutney and wild rice.

SERVES 4

Tahitian vanilla comes from a different species of vanilla orchid, "Tahitensis Moore," and is noted for its floral, fruity flavor.

SALMON WITH
VANILLA BALSAMIC MARINADE

For the marinade, combine the olive oil, shallot, parsley, basil, brown sugar, Worcestershire sauce, vinegar, Dijon mustard and vanilla paste into a blender container and purée. Pour evenly into two containers and set one container aside.

For the salmon, preheat the grill. Brush each fillet with canola oil and season with salt and pepper. Brush the tops of the fillets with the marinade, discarding any remaining marinade. Place the fillets marinated side down on a grill rack over direct heat. Grill for 6 to 8 minutes or until dark grill marks appear and the marinade begins to caramelize. Turn the fillets and grill for 3 to 4 minutes longer. Serve with the reserved marinade.

SERVES 8

VANILLA BALSAMIC MARINADE
1/4 CUP EXTRA-VIRGIN OLIVE OIL
1 SHALLOT, DICED
1 1/2 TEASPOONS DRIED ORGANIC PARSLEY
1 1/2 TEASPOONS DRIED ORGANIC BASIL
1/2 TEASPOON DARK BROWN SUGAR
1/2 TEASPOON Worcestershire SAUCE
2 TABLESPOONS BALSAMIC VINEGAR
1 TEASPOON Dijon MUSTARD
1 TEASPOON Nielsen-Massey Madagascar Bourbon Pure Vanilla Bean Paste

SALMON
8 (4- TO 6-OUNCE) 1-INCH-THICK SALMON FILLETS
~ CANOLA OIL
~ SALT AND FRESHLY GROUND PEPPER

In 1571 King Phillip II sent Francisco Hernandez on a mission to Mexico. During the six years Hernandez spent in Mexico, he became an authority on vanilla. He noted that the beans were used by the Mexicans not only for their pleasant taste and aroma, but also for their alleged healing qualities.

CRAB CAKES WITH VANILLA RÉMOULADE

Vanilla Rémoulade Sauce

1	cup mayonnaise
2	tablespoons tomato paste
1	tablespoon Nielsen-Massey Madagascar Bourbon Pure Vanilla Extract

Polenta

3	cups (or more) organic vegetable stock or chicken stock
2	tablespoons butter
1	cup polenta
~	White pepper to taste
~	Salt to taste

Crab Cakes

12	ounces canned or frozen lump crab meat
1/2	cup plain dry bread crumbs
1/4	cup mayonnaise
1	egg
1/2	cup plain dry bread crumbs
1	finely chopped green onion
3	tablespoons finely diced red bell pepper
1	teaspoon finely chopped fresh Italian parsley
1/8	teaspoon cayenne pepper
1	teaspoon salt
1/4	teaspoon black pepper
1	teaspoon Nielsen-Massey Madagascar Bourbon Pure Vanilla Extract

For the sauce, combine the mayonnaise, tomato paste and vanilla extract in a bowl and mix well. Chill, covered, in the refrigerator.

For the polenta, combine 3 cups stock, the butter and polenta in a large saucepan and stir to combine. Simmer for 15 to 20 minutes or until thick and creamy, adding additional stock if the polenta becomes too thick. Season with white pepper and salt.

For the crab cakes, rinse and drain the crab meat, discarding any shell fragments. Place 1/2 cup bread crumbs in a shallow dish. Combine the crab meat, mayonnaise, egg, 1/2 cup bread crumbs, green onion, bell pepper, parsley, cayenne pepper, salt, black pepper and vanilla extract in a large bowl and mix well. Shape into patties. Dredge in the bread crumbs to coat. Spray a nonstick skillet with oil and heat over medium-high heat. Place the crab cakes in the hot skillet and cook until crispy and golden brown.

Serve the crab cakes with the polenta and Vanilla Rémoulade Sauce.

Serves 4

VANILLA LOBSTER SUPREME WITH PASTA

Combine the stock, wine, Worcestershire sauce, vanilla extract, garlic, leek, bay leaves, nutmeg, paprika, white pepper and salt in a large saucepot. Simmer for 1 hour. Strain through a fine mesh strainer into a bowl and set aside.

Place the clarified butter in a large sauté pan over medium heat. Whisk in the flour and vanilla powder. Cook for 2 to 3 minutes, whisking constantly. Add the strained stock mixture gradually, whisking constantly. Cook for 20 minutes or until the sauce begins to thicken, stirring frequently.

Add the warm cream and lobster to the sauce. Cook until heated through. Place the pasta in a serving bowl. Spoon the lobster sauce over the pasta. Garnish with chopped parsley or freshly grated Romano cheese.

SERVES 4 TO 6

Nielsen-Massey Madagascar Bourbon Pure Vanilla Powder is alcohol free and sugar free.

4	CUPS ORGANIC VEGETABLE STOCK
1/2	CUP WHITE WINE
1/2	TEASPOON Worcestershire SAUCE
1	TABLESPOON NIELSEN-MASSEY MADAGASCAR BOURBON PURE VANILLA EXTRACT
2	WHOLE GARLIC CLOVES
1	LEEK, RINSED AND COARSELY CHOPPED
2	BAY LEAVES
1/8	TEASPOON NUTMEG
1/4	TEASPOON PAPRIKA
1/4	TEASPOON WHITE PEPPER
1	TEASPOON SALT
3	TABLESPOONS CLARIFIED BUTTER (SEE NOTE PAGE 32)
3	TABLESPOONS CAKE FLOUR
1/2	TEASPOON NIELSEN-MASSEY MADAGASCAR BOURBON PURE VANILLA POWDER
1	CUP HEAVY WHIPPING CREAM, WARMED
1 1/2	POUNDS COOKED FRESH OR THAWED FROZEN LOBSTER MEAT, COARSELY CHOPPED
~	HOT COOKED BOW TIE PASTA
~	CHOPPED PARSLEY OR FRESHLY GRATED ROMANO CHEESE FOR GARNISH

SPICY TEQUILA SHRIMP

TEQUILA MARINADE

1/4 CUP TEQUILA
2 TEASPOONS NIELSEN-MASSEY PURE MEXICAN VANILLA EXTRACT
1 SMALL STICK CINNAMON, PREFERABLY MEXICAN
3 TABLESPOONS OLIVE OIL
1 TEASPOON SALT
1/4 TEASPOON BLACK PEPPER
1/4 TEASPOON CAYENNE PEPPER (OPTIONAL)
3 GARLIC CLOVES, MINCED
3 TEASPOONS CHOPPED FRESH THYME
3 TEASPOONS CHOPPED FRESH OREGANO

SHRIMP

1 TO 1 1/2 POUNDS MEDIUM SHRIMP, PEELED AND DEVEINED
2 RED ONIONS, THINLY SLICED
1 YELLOW BELL PEPPER, THINLY SLICED
1 GREEN BELL PEPPER, THINLY SLICED
1 RED BELL PEPPER, THINLY SLICED
2 JALAPEÑO CHILES, STEMMED, SEEDED AND FINELY DICED
1 (6-OUNCE) CAN DICED TOMATOES
1/4 CUP COOL WATER
1 TABLESPOON CORNSTARCH
~ HOT COOKED RICE

For the marinade, combine the tequila, vanilla extract, cinnamon stick, olive oil, salt, black pepper, cayenne pepper, garlic, thyme and oregano in a sealable plastic bag.

For the shrimp, add the shrimp to the marinade and seal the bag, turning to coat the shrimp. Marinate in the refrigerator for 20 to 30 minutes, turning the bag occasionally. Heat a large sauté pan over medium-high heat. Add the shrimp and marinade. Sauté until the shrimp begin to change color. Add the onions, bell peppers, the jalapeño chiles and tomatoes. Cook until the vegetables are tender-crisp and shrimp turn pink.

Combine the water and cornstarch in a small cup and mix until the cornstarch is dissolved. Cook the shrimp mixture for 3 to 4 minutes. Pour in the cornstarch mixture and cook until the mixture begins to thicken.

SERVES 4 TO 6

Mexican Pure Vanilla Extract complements spice flavors such as cinnamon, ginger, nutmeg, allspice, and even savory spices such as chile peppers, thyme, and rosemary.

EGGPLANT PARMESAN

Peel the eggplant and cut crosswise into 1/4-inch-thick slices. Arrange in a single layer over a paper towel-lined baking sheet. Sprinkle with salt to sweat.

Sauté the onion and garlic in olive oil in a large saucepot until translucent. Stir in the tomatoes, tomato paste, tomato sauce, vanilla extract, cinnamon, Italian seasoning, bay leaf, 1/2 teaspoon salt and the pepper. Simmer, covered, for one hour, stirring occasionally. Remove the bay leaf.

Beat the eggs lightly in a shallow dish. Combine the flour, bread crumbs, 1 cup Parmesan cheese and the parsley in a shallow dish and mix well. Dry the eggplant slices with paper towels. Dip each slice into the eggs and then dredge in the bread crumb mixture to coat. Place on a baking sheet coated with nonstick cooking spray. Spray both sides of the eggplant slices with nonstick cooking spray. Broil on high for 2 to 3 minutes, turning when the bread crumbs turn golden brown.

Preheat the oven to 350 degrees. Coat a medium casserole with nonstick cooking spray. Cover the bottom of the dish with a small amount of the tomato sauce. Layer the eggplant, provolone and remaining sauce until all the ingredients are used, ending with the sauce. Sprinkle 1/2 cup Parmesan cheese over the top. Bake for 30 minutes or until the cheese begins to brown. Remove from the oven and let stand for 10 minutes.

Note: Sweating with salt removes the bitterness and moisture from the eggplant.

SERVES 6 TO 8

2	EGGPLANT
~	SALT
1	CUP FINELY DICED YELLOW ONION
3	GARLIC CLOVES, MINCED
2	TABLESPOONS EXTRA-VIRGIN OLIVE OIL
1	(28-OUNCE) CAN DICED TOMATOES
1	(6-OUNCE) CAN TOMATO PASTE
1	(29-OUNCE) CAN TOMATO SAUCE
1	TEASPOON NIELSEN-MASSEY ORGANIC MADAGASCAR BOURBON PURE VANILLA EXTRACT
1/4	TEASPOON CINNAMON
2	TABLESPOONS DRIED ORGANIC ITALIAN SEASONING
1	BAY LEAF
1/2	TEASPOON SALT
1/2	TEASPOON PEPPER
5	EGGS
1	CUP UNBLEACHED ALL-PURPOSE FLOUR
2	CUPS PLAIN DRY BREAD CRUMBS
1	CUP (4 OUNCES) FRESHLY GRATED PARMESAN CHEESE
2	TEASPOONS DRIED ORGANIC PARSLEY
1	POUND PROVOLONE CHEESE, SLICED
1/2	CUP (2 OUNCES) FRESHLY GRATED PARMESAN CHEESE

PASTA ARRABBIATA SAUCE

I	TABLESPOON EXTRA-VIRGIN OLIVE OIL
I 1/2	POUNDS SPICY ITALIAN SAUSAGE, CASINGS REMOVED
I	CUP FINELY DICED YELLOW ONION
4	GARLIC CLOVES, MINCED
1/2	TEASPOON CELERY SALT
I	TABLESPOON DRIED ORGANIC BASIL
2	TABLESPOONS DRIED ORGANIC OREGANO
I	BAY LEAF
I	TEASPOON SUGAR
2	TEASPOONS NIELSEN-MASSEY TAHITIAN PURE VANILLA EXTRACT
I	TEASPOON SALT
I	TEASPOON PEPPER
2	(28-OUNCE) CANS CRUSHED TOMATOES
I	(12-OUNCE) CAN TOMATO PASTE
I	(15-OUNCE) CAN TOMATO SAUCE
~	HOT COOKED PASTA

Heat the olive oil in a large saucepot over medium heat. Add the sausage and cook until brown and crumbly, stirring constantly. Remove the sausage to a paper towel-lined plate. Set aside. Add the onion to the pan drippings and sauté until golden brown. Add the garlic and sauté for 1 to 2 minutes.

Reduce the heat to low. Add the sausage, celery salt, basil, oregano, bay leaf, sugar, vanilla extract, salt and pepper. Stir in the crushed tomatoes, tomato paste and tomato sauce. Simmer for 2 hours to blend the flavors. Remove the bay leaf. Serve over your favorite pasta, prepared al dente.

SERVES 6 TO 8

Add a teaspoon of vanilla extract to tomato sauces to cut the acidity and mellow the flavor.

Extractor tanks at Chicago facility

fresh baked

VANILLA APPLE PUDDING

Preheat the oven to 350 degrees. Coat a 9×13-inch baking pan with nonstick cooking spray. Cream the butter, granulated sugar and vanilla extract in a mixing bowl using an electric mixer. Add the eggs one at a time, beating after each addition. Beat until the batter is fluffy. Add the flour, baking soda and cinnamon and mix well; the dough will be crumbly.

Add the apples and walnuts and mix just until incorporated. Press over the bottom of the prepared pan. Sprinkle the brown sugar over the top and press into the dough mixture. Bake for 30 to 35 minutes. Serve warm. Garnish with a dollop of Nielsen-Massey's Signature Whipped Cream.

SERVES 15

A few drops of Madagascar Bourbon Pure Vanilla Extract in iced tea gives a refreshingly sweet taste without sugar.

1/2 CUP (1 STICK) BUTTER, SOFTENED
2 CUPS GRANULATED SUGAR
2 TEASPOONS NIELSEN-MASSEY MADAGASCAR BOURBON PURE VANILLA EXTRACT
2 EGGS
2 CUPS UNBLEACHED ALL-PURPOSE FLOUR
2 TEASPOONS BAKING SODA
2 TEASPOONS CINNAMON
4 CUPS COARSELY CHOPPED CORED PEELED APPLES
1 CUP CHOPPED WALNUTS (OPTIONAL)
1/2 CUP FIRMLY PACKED DARK BROWN SUGAR
~ NIELSEN-MASSEY'S SIGNATURE WHIPPED CREAM FOR GARNISH (SEE PAGE 99)

VANILLA CINNAMON APPLES

4	BAKING APPLES
3	TABLESPOONS BUTTER
3/4	CUP FIRMLY PACKED DARK BROWN SUGAR
1	TEASPOON NIELSEN-MASSEY MADAGASCAR BOURBON PURE VANILLA BEAN PASTE
1 1/2	TEASPOONS CINNAMON
1/4	TEASPOON ALLSPICE
1	TABLESPOON BRANDY
1/4	CUP RAISINS
1/2	CUP WALNUTS
~	PINCH OF SALT

Preheat the oven to 350 degrees. Lightly coat the bottom of a shallow baking dish with nonstick cooking spray. Cut a thin slice from the bottom of each apple so it will stand upright. Scoop out the core of each apple from the top down with the small end of a melon ball cutter, making sure not to core all the way through the apple.

Combine the butter, brown sugar and vanilla paste in a medium saucepan and cook over low heat until the butter is melted, stirring frequently. Remove from the heat and stir in the cinnamon, allspice, brandy, raisins, walnuts and salt. Fill the apples with equal amounts of the filling using a teaspoon. Place the apples in the prepared baking dish. Bake for 20 minutes or until caramelized and fork tender.

SERVES 4

Combine Madagascar Bourbon Pure Vanilla Bean Paste with honey for a tasty, sweet spread or toss with strawberries and serve with whipped cream.

POACHED PEARS WITH VANILLA CREAM

For the pears, combine the water, sugar and lemon juice in a large saucepot. Cook over medium heat until the sugar is dissolved, stirring constantly. Remove the core of each pear starting from the bottom of the pear and using the small end of a melon ball cutter; leave the stem intact. Peel the pears and cut a thin slice from the bottom of each pear so it will stand upright. Add the pears to the water mixture, making sure they are completely submerged. Pears may need to be weighted down with a pan lid. Poach for 15 minutes or until tender. Remove from the water and let stand until cool.

For the cream, whisk the egg yolks with the sugar in a large bowl until thick and creamy. Stir in the milk and vanilla paste. Pour into the top of a double boiler and place over hot water. Cook over medium heat until the cream thickens and has an internal temperature of 160 degrees, whisking constantly. Strain through a fine mesh strainer into a bowl for a smoother cream.

Place each pear onto a dessert plate. Spoon the Vanilla Cream on the plate and over the pear.

SERVES 4

PEARS
4   CUPS WATER
3/4   CUP SUGAR
2   TABLESPOONS LEMON JUICE
4   FIRM RIPE BOSC PEARS

VANILLA CREAM
8   EGG YOLKS
1/2   CUP SUGAR
2   CUPS WHOLE MILK
1   TABLESPOON NIELSEN-MASSEY MADAGASCAR BOURBON PURE VANILLA BEAN PASTE

Queen Elizabeth I is said to have loved vanilla so much that in her later years she would not eat or drink anything unless vanilla was added.

TROPICAL FRUIT PARFAIT

8   OUNCES CREAM CHEESE, SOFTENED

3   TABLESPOONS CONFECTIONERS'
    SUGAR, SIFTED

2   TO 4 TABLESPOONS WHOLE MILK

1/2 TEASPOON NIELSEN-MASSEY PURE
    ORANGE EXTRACT

4   FRUIT CHOICES SUCH AS FINELY
    DICED MANGO, PINEAPPLE, GRAPES
    OR STRAWBERRIES OR WHOLE
    BLUEBERRIES

Combine the cream cheese, confectioners' sugar, milk and orange extract in a mixing bowl and beat using an electric mixer. Alternate layers of the cream cheese mixture and the fruit in a trifle dish or parfait glasses by either spooning the cream cheese mixture or piping with a pastry bag.

Note: Approximately 3/4 cup of each fruit choice allows for 2 tablespoons per layer in parfait glasses.

SERVES 6

Pure Orange Extract is great to flavor sugar cookies or to add to hot cocoa or chocolate milk.

VANILLA PASTRY CREAM

2/3 CUP SUGAR

1   EGG

3   EGG YOLKS

1   TEASPOON NIELSEN-MASSEY
    MADAGASCAR BOURBON PURE
    VANILLA EXTRACT

2 1/2 TABLESPOONS CORNSTARCH

1 1/2 CUPS WHOLE MILK

1/3 CUP SUGAR

2   TABLESPOONS BUTTER,
    SOFTENED

Whisk 2/3 cup sugar, the egg, egg yolks, vanilla extract and cornstarch in a bowl. Cook the milk and 1/3 cup sugar in a saucepan over medium-low heat until foam rises, stirring constantly. Remove from the heat. Temper the eggs with the hot milk mixture, stirring after each addition of the hot milk mixture (see note page 74). Pour the egg mixture into the saucepan. Cook over low heat until the pastry cream reaches 160 degrees and becomes thick, stirring constantly. Remove from the heat and whisk in the butter. Spread over parchment paper to cool.

MAKES ABOUT 1 1/2 CUPS

COFFEE CLOUD MERINGUES

Process the sugar in a miniature food processor until very fine. Preheat the oven to 225 degrees. Line a baking sheet with parchment paper.

Whip the egg whites in a nonplastic bowl using an electric mixer on medium-high speed. Whip in the coffee extract and cream of tartar. Add the sugar 1 tablespoon at a time, beating after each addition. Beat until the mixture is glossy and will hold a stiff peak.

Pipe the meringues using a pastry bag with a star tip or make dollops with a tablespoon onto the prepared baking sheet. Bake for 1 hour or until the meringues are dry. Turn off the oven and allow the meringues to cool in the oven, away from drafts, for several hours or overnight. Store in an airtight container.

MAKES 2 TO 3 DOZEN

1	CUP SUGAR
4	EGG WHITES
2	TEASPOONS NIELSEN-MASSEY PURE COFFEE EXTRACT
1/8	TEASPOON CREAM OF TARTAR

Pure Coffee Extract, when added to cocoa, makes a delicious mocha drink.

CRÈME BRÛLÉE

2 CUPS HEAVY WHIPPING CREAM
3 TABLESPOONS GRANULATED SUGAR
2 TEASPOONS NIELSEN-MASSEY MADAGASCAR BOURBON PURE VANILLA BEAN PASTE
3 EGG YOLKS
1 EGG
1/4 CUP GRANULATED SUGAR
1/8 TEASPOON SALT
1/4 CUP GRANULATED SUGAR
1/4 CUP FIRMLY PACKED LIGHT BROWN SUGAR
~ BLUEBERRIES FOR GARNISH

Preheat the oven to 325 degrees. Lightly butter six 4-ounce ramekins. Combine the cream, 3 tablespoons granulated sugar and the vanilla paste in a medium saucepan over low heat. Cook until heated through and steam is rising, stirring constantly.

Whisk the egg yolks, egg, 1/4 cup granulated sugar and the salt in a large bowl. Temper the eggs with the hot cream mixture, stirring after each addition of the hot cream mixture. Pour evenly into the ramekins.

Place the ramekins in a 9×13-inch baking pan. Fill the pan with enough hot water to reach approximately one-third of the way up the side of each ramekin. Bake for 40 to 45 minutes or until set. Let stand until cool. Chill, covered, until ready to serve.

Combine 1/4 cup granulated sugar and the brown sugar in a bowl and mix well. Sprinkle evenly over the top of each crème brûlée. Torch the top of each ramekin to caramelize the sugars or place the ramekins on a broiler pan and broil until the sugar caramelizes. Garnish with blueberries and serve.

Note: Tempering is slowly adding hot liquid to raw eggs to raise their temperature without causing them to curdle.

SERVES 6

BERRY ALMOND TART

For the dough, cream the butter, confectioners' sugar and vanilla extract in a mixing bowl using an electric mixer. Add the egg and beat until smooth. Add the flour gradually, beating on low speed until just incorporated; do not overmix. Shape into a round disk and wrap in plastic wrap. Chill until firm.

Preheat the oven to 350 degrees. Roll the dough to a 1/4-inch thickness on a lightly sugared surface, turning over once. Roll the dough up onto the rolling pin, and then place the pin across the tart pan at the center point and unroll the dough. Press the dough into the tart pan and trim the edge by rolling the pin over the pan so the dough falls freely from the edge.

For the almond cream, cream the butter, granulated sugar and almond extract in a mixing bowl using an electric mixer. Add the egg and beat until smooth. Beat in the almond flour and all-purpose flour. Spread evenly over the pastry dough. Bake for 25 to 30 minutes or until the almond cream is golden brown. Cool on a wire rack.

For the glaze, combine the granulated sugar, water and vanilla extract in a saucepan. Cook over medium heat until slightly thickened, stirring occasionally. Let stand until cooled.

To assemble, spread Vanilla Pastry Cream over the baked Almond Cream. Arrange the berries over the pastry cream. Brush the Sugar Glaze generously over the fruit. Chill until ready to serve.

SERVES 6 TO 8

PASTRY DOUGH
- 1/4 CUP (1/2 STICK) UNSALTED BUTTER, SOFTENED
- 1/2 CUP CONFECTIONERS' SUGAR
- 1 TABLESPOON NIELSEN-MASSEY MADAGASCAR BOURBON PURE VANILLA EXTRACT
- 1 EGG
- 1 3/4 CUPS UNBLEACHED ALL-PURPOSE FLOUR

ALMOND CREAM
- 1/4 CUP (1/2 STICK) UNSALTED BUTTER, SOFTENED
- 1/2 CUP GRANULATED SUGAR
- 1/4 TEASPOON NIELSEN-MASSEY PURE ALMOND EXTRACT
- 1 EGG
- 1/4 CUP ALMOND FLOUR
- 3 TABLESPOONS UNBLEACHED ALL-PURPOSE FLOUR

SUGAR GLAZE AND ASSEMBLY
- 1/3 CUP GRANULATED SUGAR
- 1/4 CUP WATER
- 1/2 TEASPOON NIELSEN-MASSEY MADAGASCAR BOURBON PURE VANILLA EXTRACT
- ~ VANILLA PASTRY CREAM (RECIPE PAGE 70)
- ~ BERRIES OF CHOICE

VANILLA-MOCHA CAFÉ CAKE

2	EGGS, LIGHTLY BEATEN
1/2	CUP CANOLA OIL
1	CUP PLAIN YOGURT
1	CUP COOLED BREWED BLACK COFFEE
2	TEASPOONS NIELSEN-MASSEY MADAGASCAR BOURBON PURE VANILLA EXTRACT
2	TEASPOONS NIELSEN-MASSEY PURE COFFEE EXTRACT
1	TEASPOON NIELSEN-MASSEY PURE CHOCOLATE EXTRACT
2	CUPS SUGAR
1 3/4	CUPS ALL-PURPOSE FLOUR
3/4	CUP UNSWEETENED COCOA
2	TEASPOONS BAKING SODA
1/2	TEASPOON SALT

Preheat the oven to 350 degrees. Coat a 12-cup Bundt pan with nonstick cooking spray.

Beat the eggs, canola oil, yogurt, coffee, vanilla extract, coffee extract and chocolate extract in a mixing bowl using an electric mixer on low speed. Add the sugar, flour, cocoa, baking soda and salt. Beat on medium speed for 2 minutes; the batter will be thin. Pour the batter into the prepared cake pan. Bake for 35 to 40 minutes or until the cake tests done. Cool in the pan on a wire rack for 15 minutes. Invert onto a serving platter. Serve with Nielsen-Massey's Cherries Jubilee Sauce.

SERVES 12 TO 16

NIELSEN-MASSEY'S CHERRIES JUBILEE SAUCE

2	(21-OUNCE) CANS SWEET CHERRIES IN HEAVY SYRUP
1/4	CUP BRANDY
1/4	CUP FIRMLY PACKED DARK BROWN SUGAR
1	TEASPOON NIELSEN-MASSEY PURE CHOCOLATE EXTRACT
2	TEASPOONS NIELSEN-MASSEY TAHITIAN PURE VANILLA EXTRACT

Combine the cherries, brandy, brown sugar, chocolate extract and vanilla extract in a large sauté pan. Cook over medium heat for 8 to 10 minutes or until the sauce thickens. Serve over Vanilla-Mocha Café Cake.

MAKES ABOUT 5 CUPS

Vanilla adds no appreciable amount of calories to dishes such as apple pie. It's a healthy way to add flavor without adding fat or sodium.

HEALTHY FRUIT NUT MUFFINS

Preheat the oven to 400 degrees. Spray twelve muffin cups with nonstick cooking spray.

Combine the flour, brown sugar, cinnamon, baking powder, baking soda and salt in a large bowl. Add the egg, yogurt, butter and vanilla powder and mix with a wooden spoon; do not overmix. Stir in the carrots, apples, pecans, raisins, cranberries and coconut; the batter will be thick.

Fill each muffin cup with 1/3 cup batter. Bake for 20 to 25 minutes or until golden brown. Cool on a wire rack.

MAKES 1 DOZEN

Sprinkle Madagascar Bourbon Pure Vanilla Powder on brownies or dust the top of a chocolate cake.

2	CUPS UNBLEACHED ALL-PURPOSE FLOUR
1/2	CUP FIRMLY PACKED DARK BROWN SUGAR
1	TEASPOON CINNAMON
1	TEASPOON BAKING POWDER
1/2	TEASPOON BAKING SODA
1/4	TEASPOON SALT
1	EGG, LIGHTLY BEATEN
1	CUP PLAIN YOGURT
1/2	CUP (1 STICK) BUTTER, MELTED
1	TEASPOON NIELSEN-MASSEY MADAGASCAR BOURBON PURE VANILLA POWDER
1/2	CUP SHREDDED CARROTS
1	CUP COARSELY CHOPPED PEELED APPLES
1	CUP COARSELY CHOPPED PECANS
1/2	CUP RAISINS
1/2	CUP DRIED CRANBERRIES
1/2	CUP COCONUT

CHEWY MACADAMIA NUT COOKIES

3/4 CUP (1 1/2 STICKS)
    BUTTER, SOFTENED
2   CUPS FIRMLY PACKED DARK
    BROWN SUGAR
1   TEASPOON NIELSEN-MASSEY
    MADAGASCAR BOURBON PURE
    VANILLA POWDER
2   EGGS
3   CUPS UNBLEACHED
    ALL-PURPOSE FLOUR
1/2 TEASPOON BAKING SODA
1/2 TEASPOON SALT
1   TEASPOON CREAM OF TARTAR
1   TEASPOON CINNAMON
1   CUP CHOPPED MACADAMIA NUTS

Cream the butter, brown sugar and vanilla powder in a mixing bowl using an electric mixer on medium speed until fluffy. Add the eggs one at a time, mixing after each addition. Add the flour, baking soda, salt, cream of tartar and cinnamon and mix well. Stir in the macadamia nuts. Chill for 2 hours.

Preheat the oven to 350 degrees. Coat an insulated cookie sheet with nonstick cooking spray.

Shape the dough into 1-inch balls and place on the prepared cookie sheet. Bake for 15 to 18 minutes or until golden brown. Cool on a wire rack.

MAKES 3 DOZEN

When preparing bakery items such as cookies, here's a tip to enhance the flavor intensity of your product: cream the vanilla into the butter or shortening and sugar first. This step encapsulates the vanilla and helps prevent flavor loss in low mass/low moisture/high heat cookies.

CRISP VANILLA BUTTER COOKIES

Cream the butter, confectioners' sugar and vanilla powder in a mixing bowl using an electric mixer on medium speed. Add the eggs and beat until light and fluffy. Beat in the flour, baking powder, cinnamon and salt on low speed until just blended. Place the dough on parchment paper and shape into a 12-inch long log. Chill for 3 to 24 hours.

Preheat the oven to 350 degrees. Coat an insulated cookie sheet with nonstick cooking spray. Cut the dough log into 1/4-inch-thick slices and place on the cookie sheet. Bake for 10 to 12 minutes or until golden brown. Cool on a wire rack. Place the cooled cookies on a parchment-lined cookie sheet.

Place the chocolate pieces in a microwave-safe bowl. Heat on High for 15 seconds. Repeat at 5-second intervals, stirring and checking the consistency. The chocolate is ready when it freely drips from the spoon in a fine line. Spoon the chocolate into a large plastic food storage bag. Twist the bag until the chocolate is in one corner and then trim the tip of the bag. Drizzle the chocolate over the cookies.

Variation: Add 1/2 teaspoon of any Nielsen-Massey Pure Flavor Extract, such as Chocolate, Almond, Lemon, Orange or Coffee, to the cookie dough to create a signature cookie.

MAKES 2 DOZEN

1	CUP (2 STICKS) BUTTER, SOFTENED
1	CUP SIFTED CONFECTIONERS' SUGAR
1	TABLESPOON NIELSEN-MASSEY MADAGASCAR BOURBON PURE VANILLA POWDER
2	EGGS, LIGHTLY BEATEN
2	CUPS UNBLEACHED ALL-PURPOSE FLOUR
1	TEASPOON BAKING POWDER
1/4	TEASPOON CINNAMON
1/4	TEASPOON SALT
1/2	CUP CHOCOLATE PIECES OF CHOICE

Pure Vanilla Powder is great for use when camping or backpacking, when a bottled liquid would be impractical.

NOT SO BLONDE BROWNIES

1 1/4 CUPS UNBLEACHED
ALL-PURPOSE FLOUR
1/4 CUP UNSWEETENED COCOA
1/2 TEASPOON BAKING SODA
1/4 TEASPOON SALT
1/2 CUP (1 STICK) BUTTER, SOFTENED
1/2 CUP FIRMLY PACKED DARK
BROWN SUGAR
1 CUP GRANULATED SUGAR
2 TEASPOONS NIELSEN-MASSEY
MADAGASCAR BOURBON PURE
VANILLA EXTRACT
3 EGGS
1/2 TEASPOON NIELSEN-MASSEY PURE
CHOCOLATE EXTRACT
2 TABLESPOONS KAHLÚA
1 CUP COARSELY CHOPPED
WHITE CHOCOLATE
3/4 CUP COARSELY CHOPPED NUTS OF
CHOICE (OPTIONAL)

Preheat the oven to 350 degrees. Sift the flour, cocoa, baking soda and salt together. Set aside.

Cream the butter, brown sugar, granulated sugar and vanilla extract in a mixing bowl using an electric mixer on medium speed. Add the eggs one at a time, beating well after each addition. Beat in the chocolate extract and Kahlúa. Add the sifted dry ingredients in two additions, beating well after each addition. Fold in the white chocolate chunks and nuts.

Spray a 9×13-inch baking pan with nonstick cooking spray. Spread the batter over the bottom of the pan with a rubber spatula. Bake for 30 to 35 minutes or until the brownies begin to pull away from the sides of the pan.

SERVES 15

Almost everything that has chocolate or chocolate flavor in it also has vanilla.

Mr. & Mrs. Richard Massey
and Dr. & Mrs. Otis Kline

it´s always better with vanilla

CRÈME BRÛLÉE FRENCH TOAST

Combine the butter, corn syrup and 1 cup brown sugar in a medium saucepan. Heat over medium heat until the butter is melted, stirring frequently. Pour over the bottom of a 1-quart baking dish coated with nonstick cooking spray. Arrange the bread slices over the brown sugar mixture so that the bread fits snugly in the dish.

Whisk the eggs, cream, salt, vanilla extract and Grand Marnier in a bowl. Pour evenly over the bread. Cover the baking dish with plastic wrap and chill for 8 hours or overnight.

Preheat the oven to 350 degrees. Sprinkle 1/2 cup brown sugar over the top of the layers. Bake for 40 to 45 minutes or until the top is golden brown.

SERVES 6

1/2 CUP (1 STICK) BUTTER
2 TABLESPOONS LIGHT CORN SYRUP
1 CUP FIRMLY PACKED LIGHT BROWN SUGAR
6 (ABOUT) SLICES ITALIAN BREAD, 1/2-INCH THICK
5 EGGS
1 1/2 CUPS HEAVY WHIPPING CREAM
1/4 TEASPOON SALT
2 TEASPOONS NIELSEN-MASSEY MADAGASCAR BOURBON PURE VANILLA EXTRACT
1 TEASPOON GRAND MARNIER
1/2 CUP FIRMLY PACKED LIGHT BROWN SUGAR

The United States consumption of vanilla beans is approximately 1,400 tons per year.

GOURMET BLUEBERRY VANILLA GRANOLA

3 1/2 CUPS OLD-FASHIONED OATS

1 CUP WHEAT GERM

3/4 CUP FLAKED COCONUT

1 CUP COARSELY CHOPPED PECANS
OR NUTS OF CHOICE

1/2 CUP FIRMLY PACKED DARK
BROWN SUGAR

1/2 CUP CANOLA OIL

1/2 CUP PURE MAPLE SYRUP

1/2 CUP GOURMET BLUEBERRY SYRUP

1 TABLESPOON NIELSEN-MASSEY
MADAGASCAR BOURBON PURE
VANILLA BEAN PASTE

2 TEASPOONS CINNAMON

1/2 TEASPOON SALT

1/2 CUP DRIED CRANBERRIES

1/2 CUP DRIED DATES

1/2 CUP RAISINS

Preheat the oven to 250 degrees. Coat a 9×13-inch baking pan with nonstick cooking spray. Combine the oats, wheat germ, coconut and pecans in a large bowl and toss to combine. Whisk the brown sugar, canola oil, maple syrup, blueberry syrup, vanilla paste, cinnamon and salt in a separate bowl. Pour over the dry ingredients and mix well.

Spread the oat mixture into the prepared pan. Bake for 50 to 60 minutes, stirring every 10 minutes. Pour the hot granola onto a large baking sheet and let stand until cool. Stir in the cranberries, dates and raisins. Store in an airtight container for up to 2 weeks.

MAKES ABOUT 10 CUPS

Stir a couple drops of Nielsen-Massey Pure Lemon Extract into blueberry yogurt and top with granola.

VANILLA CARAMEL CORN CRUNCH

Preheat the oven to 250 degrees. Pop the popcorn, discarding any unpopped kernels. Arrange the popcorn evenly in a large roasting pan. Place in the oven.

Combine the butter, brown sugar, corn syrup, vanilla paste and salt in a large saucepan. Bring to a boil slowly. Boil for 5 minutes over medium heat, stirring constantly; do not burn. Stir in the baking soda and cream of tartar, which will cause the sugar mixture to rise. Pour over the warm popcorn, stirring until coated. Bake for 1 hour, stirring every 15 minutes.

Variation: For added flavor, coarsely chop 1 cup of your favorite nuts and add to the popcorn before pouring the caramel mixture over the popcorn.

MAKES ABOUT 20 CUPS

All Nielsen-Massey products are gluten-free and safe for ingestion by people with celiac syndrome (a chronic nutritional intolerance to gluten). Vanilla beans also are naturally gluten-free.

12	OUNCES AIR-POPPED POPCORN, OR 4 (3-OUNCE) BAGS NATURAL MICROWAVE POPCORN
1	CUP (2 STICKS) BUTTER
2	CUPS FIRMLY PACKED DARK BROWN SUGAR
1/2	CUP CORN SYRUP
2	TEASPOONS NIELSEN-MASSEY MADAGASCAR BOURBON PURE VANILLA BEAN PASTE
1	TEASPOON SALT
1/2	TEASPOON BAKING SODA
1/4	TEASPOON CREAM OF TARTAR

CARAMELIZED PINEAPPLE SAUCE

1   SMALL PINEAPPLE, PEELED WITH
    EYES AND CORE REMOVED,
    SMALL DICE
1/4 CUP CLARIFIED BUTTER
    (SEE NOTE PAGE 32)
1/4 CUP FIRMLY PACKED DARK
    BROWN SUGAR
2   TABLESPOONS NIELSEN-MASSEY
    MADAGASCAR BOURBON PURE
    VANILLA BEAN PASTE

Combine the pineapple, butter, brown sugar and vanilla paste in a large sauté pan. Cook over medium heat for 5 to 8 minutes or until the pineapple is tender and the brown sugar is caramelized. Serve warm over Madagascar Vanilla Bean Ice Cream (page 112) or with Ina's Vanilla Bean Pound Cake (page 119).

MAKES ABOUT 8 TO 10 (THREE-TABLESPOON) SERVINGS

At the time of harvesting, the vanilla bean pods are green and have absolutely no characteristic vanilla flavor and aroma. It is only after the curing process, which can take up to six months, that the vanilla beans turn brown in color and the flavor and aroma that we know as "vanilla" develops.

NIELSEN-MASSEY'S SIGNATURE WHIPPED CREAMS

Whip the cream in a mixing bowl using an electric mixer on medium-high until soft peaks form. Add the coffee extract and confectioners' sugar. Whip until blended.

Add a dollop of whipped cream to a fresh cup of coffee, a dessert-style martini, a slice of rich chocolate cake or a dish of fresh fruit.

Note: Substitute Nielsen-Massey's Mexican or Tahitian Pure Vanilla Extract for the Coffee Extract, or for a unique topping try any of Nielsen-Massey's Flavored Extracts—Chocolate, Almond, Lemon, or Orange.

SERVINGS VARIABLE

Use Tahitian Pure Vanilla Extract to complement fruit desserts and pastry creams— it is a favorite among pastry chefs.

GOURMET COFFEE WHIPPED CREAM

1   CUP HEAVY WHIPPING CREAM
2   TEASPOONS NIELSEN-MASSEY PURE COFFEE EXTRACT
2   TABLESPOONS SIFTED CONFECTIONERS' SUGAR

GOURMET VANILLA WHIPPED CREAM

~   SUBSTITUTE NIELSEN-MASSEY MADAGASCAR BOURBON PURE VANILLA BEAN PASTE FOR THE COFFEE EXTRACT.

VANILLA-INFUSED SUGAR

1	NIELSEN-MASSEY MADAGASCAR BOURBON WHOLE VANILLA BEAN
2	CUPS SUGAR
~	ADDITIONAL SUGAR TO TASTE

To make vanilla-infused sugar, simply follow these four steps:

1. Split one Nielsen-Massey Madagascar Bourbon Whole Vanilla Bean in half. Scrape the seeds from each half into a glass jar.

2. Add 2 cups sugar to the vanilla seeds. Add the vanilla bean to the sugar; the bean may be cut in half.

3. Close the jar tightly and store for 1 week, shaking the jar occasionally.

4. Add additional sugar to the jar as needed. Repeat over a 6-month period or until the flavor of the vanilla bean weakens.

Use vanilla-infused sugar on cereals, French toast, fresh fruit, in coffee or in other beverages.

Note: Try Nielsen-Massey's Mexican or Tahitian Whole Vanilla Beans to create a variety of gourmet vanilla-infused sugars.

MAKES 2 CUPS

Are vanilla pods, or beans, as they are commonly called, the fruit of an orchid? Yes— of the thousands of varieties of the orchid, the vanilla plant is the only one with an edible fruit. It is a small, trumpet-shaped greenish, white flower which grows on a vine.

VANILLA MAPLE SYRUP

Combine the syrup and vanilla extract in a small saucepan and mix well. Heat until warm.

Note: Substitute Nielsen-Massey's Mexican or Tahitian Pure Vanilla Extract for a change of taste.

MAKES 1 CUP

1 CUP PURE MAPLE SYRUP
2 TEASPOONS NIELSEN-MASSEY MADAGASCAR BOURBON PURE VANILLA EXTRACT

A tiny bee, the Melipone, found only in Mexico was historically responsible for the pollination of the orchid. For over three hundred years, after its discovery by Europeans, vanilla pods were produced only in Mexico because of this bee. Vines were grown successfully in other parts of the world, where they flowered beautifully, but only a small number of pods appeared, inadvertently pollinated by insects.

DELICIOUS VANILLA HONEY BUTTER

1/2   CUP (1 STICK) BUTTER, SOFTENED
2   TABLESPOONS SIFTED
    CONFECTIONERS' SUGAR
1   TABLESPOON HONEY
1   TEASPOON NIELSEN-MASSEY
    MADAGASCAR BOURBON PURE
    VANILLA EXTRACT

Combine the butter, confectioners' sugar, honey and vanilla extract in a mixing bowl. Beat using an electric mixer until creamy.

Use on pancakes, waffles, cornbread, biscuits, popovers or scones.

Note: Substitute Nielsen-Massey's Mexican or Tahitian Pure Vanilla Extract and create new butter flavors.

MAKES 1/2 CUP

In 1841 a former slave, Edmond Albious, of the Island of Reunion, devised a practical and speedy method of fertilizing the flower by hand. This method is still in use today. Pollination by hand is actually an improvement over nature in that the best flowers, properly spaced, can be chosen.

VANILLA OIL

Combine the canola oil and vanilla extract in a bowl and whisk to blend. Store, covered, in the refrigerator for up to 2 weeks.

Brush over grilled vegetables or fruits such as pineapple or papaya.

Note: For additional flavored oils, try Nielsen-Massey's Organic Madagascar Bourbon Pure Vanilla Extract, Mexican Pure Vanilla Extract, or Tahitian Pure Vanilla Extract.

MAKES 1/2 CUP

1/2 CUP CANOLA OIL
1 TEASPOON NIELSEN-MASSEY MADAGASCAR BOURBON PURE VANILLA EXTRACT

Vanilla, with more than three hundred flavor components, is native to Mexico along with chocolate, chiles, and corn.

Sorting and bundling Mexican vanilla beans

(chef) hats off to vanilla

CHERRY VANILLA CHICKEN À LA NIELSEN

Soak the cherries in the vanilla extract in a bowl for 10 minutes. Rinse and pat dry the chicken. Cut a pocket in the thickest part of each chicken breast. Spoon 1/2 tablespoon of the vanilla paste into each pocket and stuff with the marinated cherries, reserving some for the sauce. Secure each pocket closed with two wooden picks.

Preheat the oven to 350 degrees. Season the chicken with salt and pepper. Heat the olive oil in an ovenproof skillet. Sauté the chicken in the hot oil over medium-high heat until golden brown on each side. Sprinkle with the rosemary. Bake for 20 to 25 minutes or to 165 degrees on a meat thermometer.

Remove the chicken from the skillet and place one on each of four dinner plates. Remove the wooden picks. Place the skillet over medium-high heat. Pour the wine into the skillet, scraping the bottom of the pan with a wooden spoon, to deglaze the pan (see note page 31). Add the reserved cherries and vanilla extract. Cook until the liquid is reduced. Spoon approximately 2 tablespoons of the cherries and sauce over each chicken breast.

Note: Reduce is when a liquid is cooked until the liquid amount decreases and thickens, which intensifies the flavor.

SERVES 4

Contributed by Chef J. Warren, CJW Productions
Thank you, J. Warren, from the Nielsen Family

3/4	CUP DRIED CHERRIES, COARSELY CHOPPED
1/3	CUP NIELSEN-MASSEY MADAGASCAR BOURBON PURE VANILLA EXTRACT
4	BONELESS SKINLESS CHICKEN BREASTS
2	TABLESPOONS NIELSEN-MASSEY MADAGASCAR BOURBON PURE VANILLA BEAN PASTE
~	SALT AND FRESHLY GROUND PEPPER TO TASTE
2	TABLESPOONS OLIVE OIL
2	TEASPOONS MINCED FRESH ROSEMARY
1	CUP DRY WHITE WINE

MADAGASCAR VANILLA BEAN ICE CREAM

2   NIELSEN-MASSEY MADAGASCAR
    BOURBON WHOLE VANILLA BEANS
1   TEASPOON NATURAL FRUIT PECTIN
1/4   CUP SUGAR
2 1/2   CUPS WHOLE MILK
3   TABLESPOONS MILK POWDER
    (0% MILK FAT)
1/2   CUP SUGAR
1/4   CUP HONEY
1 1/2   CUPS HEAVY WHIPPING
    CREAM (35% FAT)
2   EGG YOLKS

Split the vanilla beans in half and scrape the seeds from each half into a large saucepan. Add the beans. Combine the pectin and 1/4 cup sugar in a bowl and mix to combine.

Add the milk and milk powder to the saucepan. Add 1/2 cup sugar, the honey, cream and egg yolks. Add the pectin mixture. Cook over medium heat to a maximum of 185 degrees, whisking constantly. Remove from the heat and cool in an ice bath until the mixture reaches 39 degrees.

Chill, covered for 12 hours. Strain the mixture and pour into an ice cream freezer container. Freeze using the manufacturer's directions.

MAKES 1 QUART

Contributed by The French Pastry School at
City Colleges of Chicago
Thank you, from the Nielsen Family

FLAN CLÁSICO DE VANILLA

Sprinkle the water over 3/4 cup sugar in a small saucepan. Bring to a boil over medium-high heat. Brush down the side of the pan with a brush dipped in water to dissolve any sugar crystals. Reduce the heat to medium. Boil for 3 to 5 minutes or until golden in color; do not stir. Swirl the caramel in the saucepan gently until it becomes a deep straw color. Remove from the heat. Swirl the caramel until amber in color. Pour even amounts into each of six 6-ounce or four 8-ounce molds, tilting the molds to evenly cover the bottoms.

Position a rack in the middle of the oven and preheat to 325 degrees. Combine the milk, 1/4 cup sugar, the condensed milk and lime zest in a saucepan. Bring to a simmer, stirring frequently. Remove from the heat. Steep, covered, for 10 minutes. Whisk the eggs and yolks in a bowl. Whisk in the warm milk mixture a little at a time. Stir in the vanilla extract. Strain through a fine mesh strainer into a glass measuring cup.

Place the molds 1/2 inch apart in a deep baking pan. Pour 2 inches of hot water into the baking pan. Pour the custard mixture into the molds. Bake for 50 to 60 minutes. Remove from the oven. Let cool in the hot water bath. Chill for 2 hours before serving. Run a sharp knife along the top edge of the molds to loosen the custards. Invert onto dessert plates.

SERVES 6 TO 8

*Contributed by Rick Bayless, Chef and Owner
of Frontera Grill/Topolobampo in Chicago
Host of "Mexico—One Plate at a Time"
Thank you, Rick, from the Nielsen Family*

1/3	CUP WATER
3/4	CUP GRANULATED SUGAR
1 1/2	CUPS MILK
1/4	CUP GRANULATED SUGAR
1	(14-OUNCE) CAN SWEETENED CONDENSED MILK
4	(1/2×2-INCH) STRIPS OF LIME ZEST (OPTIONAL)
3	EGGS
4	EGG YOLKS
1 1/2	TEASPOONS NIELSEN-MASSEY PURE MEXICAN VANILLA EXTRACT

VANILLA-ALMOND PANNA COTTA WITH APRICOT SAUCE

PANNA COTTA

1 TABLESPOON GELATIN
1/4 CUP BOILING WATER
1 1/2 CUPS HEAVY WHIPPING CREAM
1 TABLESPOON NIELSEN-MASSEY MADAGASCAR BOURBON PURE VANILLA EXTRACT
1/3 CUP ALMOND SYRUP, SUCH AS ORZATA

APRICOT SYRUP

1 CUP SUGAR
1/2 CUP WATER
1 TABLESPOON NIELSEN-MASSEY MADAGASCAR BOURBON PURE VANILLA EXTRACT
5 FRESH APRICOTS, HALVED, PEELED AND PITTED
~ CANDIED ALMONDS FOR GARNISH

For the panna cotta, dissolve the gelatin in the boiling water in a small heatproof bowl. Heat the cream and vanilla extract in a medium saucepan until warm. Fold in the syrup and dissolved gelatin. Pour equal amounts into each of four to six dessert molds. Chill, covered, for 4 to 5 hours or until firm.

For the syrup, combine the sugar, water, vanilla extract and apricots in a medium saucepan. Cook over medium heat until the mixture has the consistency of thick syrup, stirring occasionally. Remove from the heat and let stand until room temperature. Purée in a blender. Strain the mixture through a fine mesh strainer into a glass bowl.

Spoon the Apricot Syrup over the panna cotta and garnish with candied almonds.

SERVES 4 TO 6

Contributed by Chef Biagio Settepani, Owner of Bruno Bakery & Pasticceria Bruno in New York Thank you, Biagio, from the Nielsen Family

INA'S VANILLA BEAN POUND CAKE

Position a rack in the middle of the oven and preheat to 350 degrees. Butter and flour a 5×9-inch loaf pan. Sift the cake flour, baking powder and salt into a medium bowl. Combine the sugar, eggs and vanilla paste in a food processor container and process for 5 seconds.

Melt the butter slowly in a microwave-safe measuring cup or in a saucepan on the stove. Stir the butter to combine the milk solids with the butter fat. Pour the butter through the food processor feed tube in a slow steady stream, processing constantly. Spoon the sugar mixture into a large bowl. Fold in the sifted dry ingredients in three stages until just combined.

Pour the batter into the prepared pan. Bake for 15 minutes. Reduce the temperature to 325 degrees. Bake for an additional 35 to 40 minutes or until golden brown, rotating the pan halfway through the baking time. Cool in the pan for 10 minutes. Invert onto a wire rack to cool.

SERVES 6

Contributed by Chef Ina Pinkney, Owner of Ina's in Chicago
Thank you, Ina, from the Nielsen Family

1 1/2 CUPS CAKE FLOUR
1 TEASPOON BAKING POWDER
1/2 TEASPOON SALT
1 1/4 CUPS SUGAR
4 EGGS
1 TABLESPOON NIELSEN-MASSEY MADAGASCAR BOURBON PURE VANILLA BEAN PASTE
1 CUP (2 STICKS) UNSALTED BUTTER

MARCY'S VANILLA SUGAR-CRUSTED SCONES

1	Nielsen-Massey Madagascar Bourbon Vanilla Bean
3	cups all-purpose flour
1	tablespoon baking powder
1/3	cup sugar
1/2	teaspoon salt
3/4	cup (1 1/2 sticks) unsalted butter, cut into small cubes
1	egg
2	teaspoons Nielsen-Massey Madagascar Bourbon Pure Vanilla Extract
1	cup (or less) whipping cream
1/2	cup sugar
1/2	cup (1 stick) unsalted butter, melted

Position an oven rack in the upper third of the oven and preheat to 400 degrees. Line two baking sheets with parchment paper. Cut the vanilla bean lengthwise and scrape the seeds into a bowl; discard the bean. Combine the flour, baking powder, 1/3 cup sugar and the salt in a food processor container and process for 10 seconds.

Add equal amounts of the butter in three stages to the dry ingredients and process for 6 to 8 seconds per addition; the dough should have a slightly coarse texture. Place the dough in a large mixing bowl and make a well in the center. Add the egg, vanilla extract, 3/4 cup of the cream and the vanilla seeds. Stir with a fork ten to fourteen times while turning the bowl. Knead five or six times; the dough should hold together. Add enough of the remaining cream to reach the desired consistency if the dough does not hold together or seems dry.

Sprinkle 1/2 cup sugar on a work surface. Turn the dough onto the sugared work surface and knead gently so the dough holds together. Let rest for 3 to 5 minutes. Divide the dough into two discs 1-inch thick and 6 to 8 inches in diameter. Cut into wedges. Place the scones on the prepared pans. Brush with the butter. Bake for 17 to 20 minutes or until brown. Remove to a wire rack to cool.

MAKES 1 TO 1 1/2 DOZEN

This is a Marcy Goldman/www.BetterBaking.com original recipe.
Thank you, Marcy, from the Nielsen Family

LEMON-PISTACHIO BISCOTTI

Preheat the oven to 350 degrees. Line two large baking sheets with foil or Silpat nonstick baking sheets. Combine the flour, baking powder and salt in a large bowl and mix well. Combine the brandy and lemon extract in a small bowl and mix well. Beat the sugar and butter in a large mixing bowl using an electric mixer until fluffy. Add the eggs one at a time, beating well after each addition. Add the flour mixture alternately with the brandy mixture, beginning and ending with the flour mixture and mixing well after each addition. Add the pistachios and lemon zest and mix well.

Divide the dough into four equal portions. Drop spoonfuls of dough from one portion across a baking sheet to form a 2-inch wide-line with a length of 13 inches. Repeat with the remaining dough portions. Shape the dough into smooth logs. Bake for 35 to 40 minutes or until golden brown and firm to the touch. Remove from the oven. Cool on the baking sheets on wire racks.

Reduce the oven temperature to 300 degrees. Move the logs to a cutting board. Cut on the diagonal into 3/4-inch-thick slices. Arrange the slices on the baking sheets, cut sides down. Bake for 20 to 30 minutes or until dry and slightly brown, turning after 10 minutes. Biscotti can be made two weeks ahead and stored in an airtight container at room temperature.

MAKES 4 DOZEN

Contributed by Todd Eller
Thank you, Todd, from the Nielsen Family

4 1/2 CUPS ALL-PURPOSE FLOUR
4 TEASPOONS BAKING POWDER
1 TEASPOON SALT
1/3 CUP BRANDY*
1 1/2 TEASPOONS NIELSEN-MASSEY PURE LEMON EXTRACT
2 CUPS SUGAR
1 CUP (2 STICKS) UNSALTED BUTTER, SOFTENED
4 EGGS
1 CUP SHELLED PISTACHIOS, COARSELY CHOPPED AND TOASTED
2 TABLESPOONS FINELY GRATED LEMON ZEST (ABOUT 1 LEMON)

You may substitute 1/4 cup Lemoncella for the brandy to produce a much sweeter cookie.

TO THE CUSTOMERS OF
NIELSEN-MASSEY
VANILLAS
MANY THANKS
AND MERRY XMAS
FROM THE USO AND
SERVICEMEN IN
VIET-NAM

INDEX

INDEX

For more information about
Nielsen-Massey Vanillas, Inc.
and all of our products,
please call 800-525-PURE (7873)
OR
visit our Web site at
www.nielsenmassey.com.